Philosophy and Philosophers

Author: Lois Roets Ed.D.

ZEPHYR PRESS
3316 North Chapel Avenue
Tucson, AZ 85716-1416
P.O. Box 13448
Tucson, AZ 85732-3448
(602) 322-5090
FAX (602) 323-9402

Table of Contents

PHILOSOPHY AND PHILOSOPHERS

PHILOSOPHY AND PHILOSOPHERS copyright, 1987, Lois Roets Ed.D.

ISBN: 0-911943-12-9

LEADERSHIP PUBLISHERS
Promoting Leadership & Human Potential
Div. of Roets Publications 515-637-4563
407 West Cherry Street, P.O. Box 51
New Sharon, IA 50207

Philosophy

<u>Philosophy</u> is the study of wisdom. Wisdom gives meaning to daily events and interprets periods of time.

Philosophy considers everything people know, think, feel, desire or hope. Philosophers are those who ponder eternal questions. The answers they give are philosophy.

Origin of word "Philosophy"

The word <u>philosophy</u> comes from two Greek words:

philia — to love
sophia — wisdom

therefore:
a <u>philosopher</u> is a "lover of wisdom"
<u>philosophy</u> is the "study of wisdom".

Read and Interpret a Scenario.

*~ The philosophy of a person or culture can be judged by ~
the attitudes held and the actions performed.*

Directions: Read the SCENARIO. Consider the INTERPRETATION items.

The SCENARIO. **the PARTY**

Dimitri's invitation said "Come to My Party".

Nick wondered: Should he go to the party? Dimitri had a reputation, or so Nick had heard, for having wild parties.

But Mitty — as Dimitri's friends called him — could be a lot of fun. He was popular.

Sara, Nick's girlfriend, didn't like Dimitri. "There's something about him I don't like."

INTERPRETING the scenario:

*If you were Nicholas, which decision would be yours?
Check one and give your reason(s).*

_____ *go to Dimitri's party alone.*

_____ *go to Dimitri's party with Sara.*

_____ *decline the invitation.*

REASON(S):

____

____

____

____

____

THE GOLDEN RULE

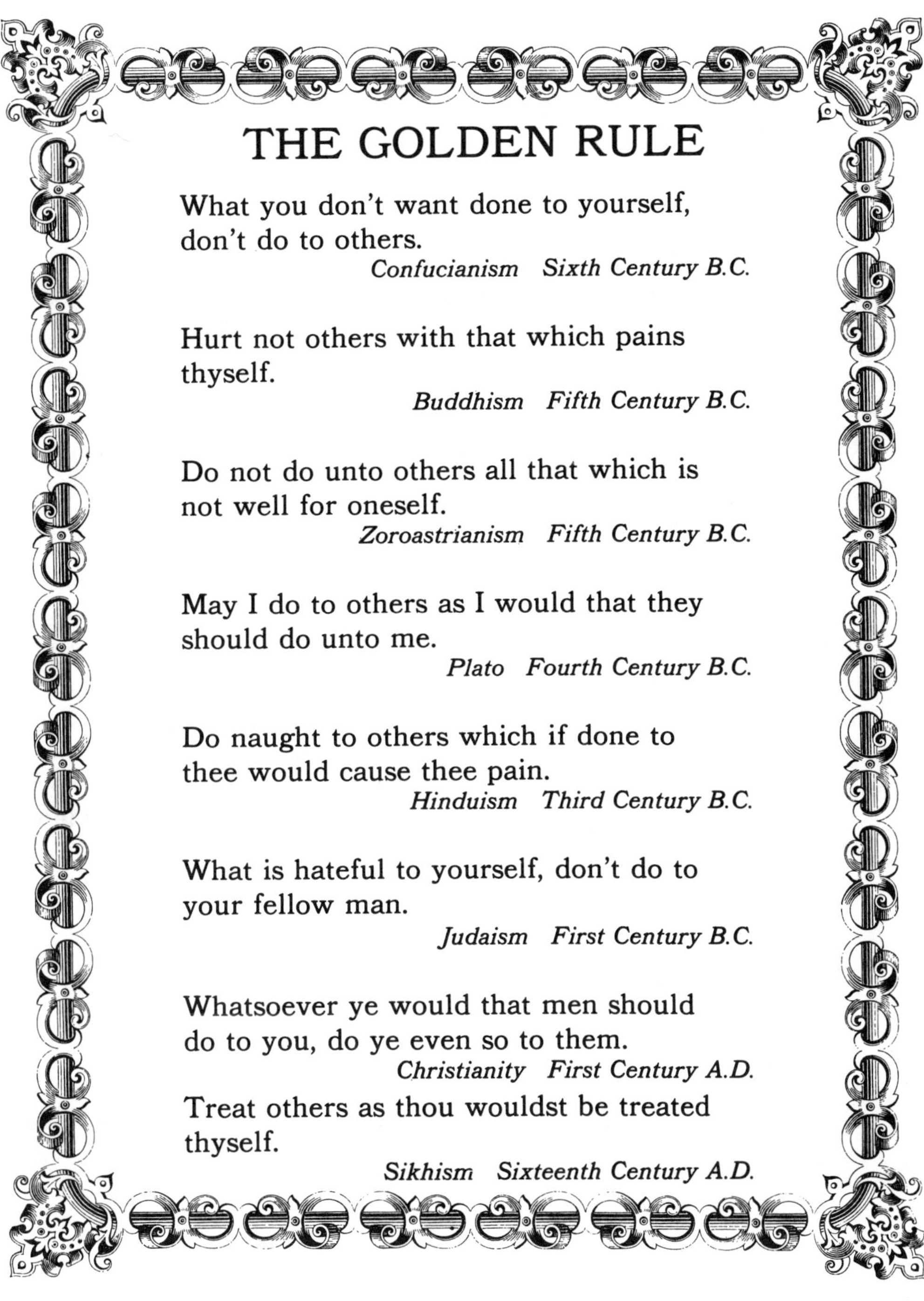

What you don't want done to yourself, don't do to others.

Confucianism   Sixth Century B.C.

Hurt not others with that which pains thyself.

Buddhism   Fifth Century B.C.

Do not do unto others all that which is not well for oneself.

Zoroastrianism   Fifth Century B.C.

May I do to others as I would that they should do unto me.

Plato   Fourth Century B.C.

Do naught to others which if done to thee would cause thee pain.

Hinduism   Third Century B.C.

What is hateful to yourself, don't do to your fellow man.

Judaism   First Century B.C.

Whatsoever ye would that men should do to you, do ye even so to them.

Christianity   First Century A.D.

Treat others as thou wouldst be treated thyself.

Sikhism   Sixteenth Century A.D.

Discuss: The "Golden Rule" has existed for many centuries and in many cultures. Why, then, are there wars which cause pain and suffering?

Name: *Confucius*

Biographical Information:

551 (?) - 479 (?) B.C.
Confucius was born in the duchy of Lu in what is now Shantung Province, China. His real name was K'ung Chi'iu. The name "Confucius" was a Latin form of the title "K'ung-fu-'tzu" which means "Great Master K'ung".

Contribution to Philosophy:

Confucius is perhaps the most influential and respected philosopher in Chinese history. From the 100's B.C. to the 1900's A.D., his ideas have had a strong influence on Chinese way of life.

In the time of Confucius, China was made up of many independent states. Constant wars continuously changed the political and social structure of China. Confucius thought that these wars were a threat to an orderly society. They would destroy civilization.

To save society and civilization, Confucius emphasized sincerity in personal and public conduct, strong moral character, and devoted respect to fathers and ruler. A person was to exercise good thinking, and choose to act according to definite rules of conduct.

Confucius felt that virtuous behavior of rulers provided a role model for the rest of the country. Leaders should rule by correct behavior rather than rule by laws and punishments.

No book exists that was definitely written by Confucius. His conversations and sayings were recorded by his disciples in a book called ANALECTS.

These thoughts are from Confucius:

"Do not wish for quick results, nor look for small advantages. If you seek quick results, you will not attain the ultimate goal. If you are led astray by small advantages, you will never accomplish great things."

"The nobler man first practices what he preaches and afterwards preaches according to his practice."

"To go too far is as bad as to fall short."

The Philosopher: Attitudes and Tools

A philosopher usually holds these attitudes:
1. A belief in one's mental powers.
2. A habit of questioning ideas, theories, and practices.
3. An inquisitive mind that is always asking "why"?
4. A global view of the universe.

Others:

____

____

____

____

____

A philosopher uses these tools:
1. Logic and reason.
2. Intuition.
3. Observation
4. Discussion.
5. Synthesis of many bits of information.

Others:

____

____

____

____

Read and Interpret a Scenario

*✳ The philosophy of a person or culture can be judged by ✳
the attitudes held and the actions performed.*

Directions: Read the SCENARIO. Consider the INTERPRETATION items.

The SCENARIO **The Prairie** 

The wind had blown for many days. At the end of another hot summer day, Mary and John, the mother and father, were sitting near their sod home. The dust from the dry land occasionally swirled onto their faces.

"Does that cloud look like a rain cloud?" Mary asked, as she pointed to a wisp of white in the distance.

"Can't tell until it comes closer," replied John.

Both sat in silence.

John looked at their son, Adam, playing in the yard. "I'll need Adam tomorrow afternoon. The fields need work."

She paused and then replied, "He puts in three hours already each day in the field. I think a growing boy needs free time to play and explore.

"He needs play, but the fields need work," said John.

"I need him, too," Mary replied softly. "He keeps me company. The house is lonely when you are out in the fields all day."

"I see," said John.

After a bit he spoke. "I could do the afternoon fieldwork if Adam would take over a few more evening chores. What do you think?"

"Splendid!"

She gently touched his arm. Then she looked into the yard where Adam was playing his own version of one-man soccer.

INTERPRETING the scenario

1. HOW DO MARY AND JOHN VIEW THEIR LIFE ON THE PRAIRIE?

2. WHAT PATTERN OF DECISION-MAKING HAS BEEN ESTABLISHED IN REGARD TO RAISING OF ADAM, THE TEN-YEAR-OLD SON?

3. DO JOHN AND MARY BELIEVE THAT A CHILD HAS AN OBLIGATION TO CONTRIBUTE TO THE GENERAL SUCCESS OF A FAMILY?

4. DOES THE MOTHER CONSIDER HER LIFE WORTHWHILE?

5. DOES THE FATHER CONSIDER HIS LIFE WORTHWHILE?

6. DO YOU THINK A SCENE LIKE THIS COULD HAPPEN?

6

Read and Interpret a Scenario

** The philosophy of a person or culture can be judged by *
the attitudes held and the actions performed.*

Directions: Read the SCENARIO. Consider the INTERPRETATION items.

The SCENARIO HERITAGE

Once a year Thomas put on the feathered headdress of his native tribe. Once a year, Thomas became "Swift Feather" — a member of the ancient noble tribe of nomadic hunters.

Thomas gently touched the feathers. A few feathers were losing their firmness. He'd replace those this year.

"Let me put it on," begged Jessie, his five year-old daughter.

Thomas carefully and gently placed the feathered headdress on her head. He said, "You are now 'Running Doe', daughter of the chief."

She touched the feathers. Both were silent.

Thomas removed the headdress. He held his young daughter in his arms.

"Never forget," he said, "that you came from a great people."

INTERPRETING the scenario

1. HOW IMPORTANT IS CULTURAL HERITAGE TO THE INDIVIDUAL?

2. IS THOMAS PROUD OF HIS HERITAGE?

3. DO YOU THINK JESSIE WILL BE PROUD OF HER HERITAGE?

4. WHAT DETERMINES HERITAGE?
   (geography, bloodlines...?)

Read and Interpret a Scenario

> *The philosophy of a person or culture can be judged by the attitudes held and the actions performed.*

Directions: Read the SCENARIO. Consider the INTERPRETATION items.

The SCENARIO Death

Brother Francis walked behind the burial casket. His friend, Brother Leo, was dead.

He and Brother Leo had worked together in the fields, in the kitchen, in the laundry. During evening recreation, they had shared humorous events that had happened throughout the day. They had laughed and talked together.

Now Brother Leo was gone.

Brother Francis felt tears in his eyes. He was glad Brother Leo had gone to his heavenly reward. But he, Brother Francis, had lost his best friend.

INTERPRETING the scenario

1. DOES BROTHER FRANCIS BELIEVE IN AN EXISTENCE AFTER DEATH?

2. WHAT IS FRIENDSHIP?

3. DOES A BURIAL SERVICE (CEREMONY OR RITE) MEET THE NEEDS OF THE <u>LIVING</u> OR THE <u>DEAD</u>?

4. WHAT IS THE PURPOSE OF EXISTENCE?

Name: SOCRATES

Biographical Information:

469 (?) - 399 B.C.   Athens, Greece
Condemned to death by drinking poison hemlock.

Contribution to Philosophy:

Socrates spent much of his life thinking and discussing.

Socrates taught in the streets and market place. He taught by questioning his listeners and showing them how inadequate their answers were.

He believed that by arguing intelligently, one could discover truth. This method has come to be known as the <u>Socratic Method</u>.

Socrates felt that evil and wrong actions arise from ignorance. He felt that the correct method of thinking was reasoning from particular facts to a general idea.

Socrates was one of the first to popularize the maxim ''A sound mind in a sound body.''

He was charged with corruption of the youth of Athens and disrespect for religious traditions. He was found guilty and sentenced to death by drinking poison hemlock. He willingly did so rather than withdraw his ideas.

Socrates did not write down his teachings. We know of them through the writings of others. He is credited with these ideas:

"I am not an Athenian nor a Greek, but a citizen of the world."

"The unexamined life is not worth living."

> *"A sound mind in a sound body."*

9

PLATO

Plato was a nickname meaning "broad-shouldered".
His real name was Aristocles.

Biographical Information:

427 (?) – 347 (?) B.C.   Athens,Greece
Son of a wealthy and noble Athenian family.

Contribution to Philosophy:

As a young man, Plato wanted to be a politician. But he was disgusted with many political actions of his day.

In 404 B.C. a group of wealthy men, including two of Plato's relatives, established themselves as dictators in Athens. They invited Plato to join them. He refused because he was disgusted with their cruel and unethical actions.

In 403 B.C., when the Athenians overthrew the dictators and established a democracy, Plato again considered politics. But his friend, the philosopher Socrates, was brought to trial and sentenced to death in 399 B.C. He was again disgusted with politics. He left Athens and traveled extensively for several years.

In 387 B.C. Plato returned to Athens to start his school, called the ACADEMY. Subjects taught were: philosophy, astronomy, biological sciences, mathematics, and political science.

He felt that immoral behavior is a sign of a diseased soul.

Plato's writing followed the <u>dialogue</u> form. A dialogue is a conversation between two or more people. The characters discuss ideas.

One of Plato's works is the REPUBLIC, a description of the ideal society. The central issue in the REPUBLIC is "What is justice?".

Plato's ideas influenced thinkers from his time even to the present day.

"Those having torches will pass them on to others."

"Philosophy is the highest music."

10

Name: ARISTOTLE

Biographical Information:

384 - 322 B.C.
Born in Stagira, a small town in northern Greece.
His father was court physician to the king of Macedon.

Contribution to Philosophy:

Aristotle studied in Plato's school, the ACADEMY. He stayed there with Plato for 20 years. When Plato died, he left the ACADEMY.

Aristotle believed that a good person avoids extremes and tries to live in a moderate manner. He called his notion ''The Golden Mean''.

Aristotle believed that man is a ''political animal''. He believed that man must play an important role within the society in which he lives.

Aristotle's book, POETICS, examines the nature of tragedy. Aristotle believed that tragedy, in a drama or novel, affects the spectator by arousing the emotions of pity and fear. Then, tragedy purifies and cleanses the spectator of these emotions.

One of Aristotle's students was Alexander, later to become Alexander the Great. Alexander conquered all of Greece. Alexander and Aristotle were friends.

The citizens of Athens did not like Aristotle because he was a friend of Alexander, the ruler who conquered them. Soon after Alexander died, Aristotle was charged with ''impiety'' by the citizens of Athens.

Aristotle remembered the fate of Socrates whom the Athenians forced to drink poison hemlock.

Aristotle fled Athens so that the city would not ''sin twice against philosophy''.

He died a year later.

The "...isms"

EMPIRICISM—a theory that all knowledge comes from experience.

HEDONISM—a theory that tells people to seek pleasure.

IDEALISM—a theory that things exist only in the mind.

NATURALISM—a theory that everything is natural and that nothing exists outside of nature.

RATIONALISM—a theory that knowledge comes only from logical and deductive reasoning.

REALISM—a theory that things exist in and of themselves.

Discuss:
1. *Do you think a hedonist would go on a hunger strike?*
2. *Do you think a rationalist would conduct scientific experiments?*
3. *Do you think an empiricist would conduct scientific experiments?*

Write another question. ______________________________

____

Answer the question. ______________________________

____

The "...ologies"

"...ology" means "the study of..."

ASTROLOGY—the study of the supposed influence of heavenly bodies on human concerns.

AXIOLOGY—the study of values.

COSMOLOGY—the study of the universe as an integrated whole.

EPISTEMOLOGY—the study of knowledge.

IDEOLOGY—the study of the beliefs of a group.

ONTOLOGY—the study of the nature of existence.

PSYCHOLOGY—the study of the mind and spirit.

Activity:
1. List other "...ologies" and their definitions,
or
2. Create words using "...ology", meaning "the study of".
Example: TEENOLOGY—the study of teenagers.

Education

AXIOLOGY—the study of values.

VALUES DICTATE MANY OF OUR ACTIONS AND ATTITUDES.

VALUES INFLUENCE EVERY ASPECT OF OUR LIFE.

Answer this question:

According to your values, what is the importance
of education?

____

____

____

____

____

____

Matching . . . ologies and . . . isms

astrology   axiology   cosmology   empiricism   epistemology
hedonism   idealism   ideology   naturalism   ontology
psychology   rationalism   realism

1. _______________________ a theory that tells people to seek pleasure.

2. _______________________ a theory that things exist in and of themselves.

3. _______________________ the study of the beliefs of a group.

4. _______________________ a theory that all knowledge comes from experience.

5. _______________________ the study of the universe as an integrated whole.

6. _______________________ the study of the mind and spirit.

7. _______________________ a theory that knowledge comes only from logical and deductive reasoning.

8. _______________________ the study of values.

9. _______________________ a theory that everything is natural and that nothing exists outside of nature.

10. _______________________ the study of the supposed influence of heavenly bodies on human concerns.

11. _______________________ the study of knowledge.

12. _______________________ a theory that things exist only in the mind.

13. _______________________ the study of the nature of existence.

Name: *Rene Descartes*

Biographical Information:

1596-1650.   Born in Touraine, France.
He was a weak child who was permitted no strenous exercise.
His mother died when he was very small.
His father raised him.

Contribution to Philosophy:

Many scholars consider Rene Descartes to be the father of modern philosophy. He emphasized the use of reason as the chief tool of thought.

Descartes thought that the chief task of philosophy was to analyze complex ideas and put them into simpler ones. Each new thought refinement should produce clearer, more distinct ideas.

He applied reason to philosophy, mathematics, and science. Mathematics fascinated Rene because it was so clear and distinct.

For Descartes, thinking always started with a doubt which was then resolved. There was one thing he didn't doubt — his own existence. He expressed this belief in the now-famous quotation:

''I think; therefore I am.''

Descartes believed reality has a dual nature: <u>mind</u> (intellect and spirit) and <u>matter</u> (observable substance).

His most famous written work is DISCOURSE ON THE METHOD OF RIGHTLY CONDUCTING THE REASON AND SEEKING FOR TRUTH IN THE SCIENCES.

Name: John Locke

Biographical Information:

1632-1704. Born in Wrington in Somerset County, England. His father was a prominent country lawyer.

Contribution to Philosophy:

John Locke was a man of many interests: theology, medicine, physics, chemistry, and politics. He knew many of the leading people of his time.

As secretary to the British Ambassador, Locke traveled extensively for 4 years. A violent asthma attack forced him to give up traveling.

Locke believed that, at the time of birth, a mind is a <u>tabula rasa</u> — a blank sheet of paper. Our experiences fill in the <u>tabula rasa</u>.

There are, according to Locke, two kinds of experiences:
1. OUTER EXPERIENCE by which we learn through our senses.
2. INNER EXPERIENCE in which we learn by thinking about what we learned through the Outer Experience.

Because Locke believed that we learn through personal experiences, he is considered the founder of modern psychology.

Locke believed that people, by nature, have certain rights and duties. The rights are: liberty, life, and ownership of property. He felt that if rulers did not adequately protect the rights of citizens, the citizens had the right to find other rulers.

Locke's book TWO TREATISES OF GOVERNMENT greatly influenced Thomas Jefferson.

> *"We should have a great many fewer disputes in the world if words were taken for what they are, the signs of our ideas only, and not for things themselves."*

Read and Interpret a Scenario.

The philosophy of a person or culture can be judged by the attitudes held and the actions performed.

Directions:

Read the SCENARIO. Consider the INTERPRETATION items.

The SCENARIO **Polar Bears**

The scientists looked at the huge polar bear.

"It's a big one," said Josh, head of POLAR BEAR RESEARCH.

"How old do you think it is?" asked Jake, his assistant.

"We can't be certan until we verify. I'll estimate the bear is about eight years old. Pull out that back tooth."

Jake positioned the forceps around the back molar. He yanked out the tooth. He placed it into a plastic bag labeled "Bear 12". He wrote the date, location, length and girth of the bear's body, size of the skull, and other bits of information onto the label.

"Let's hurry and put that identifying tattoo on the upper lip. I want to get home," said Josh.

The men hurried to complete the job on Bear 12.

The tooth would be sent for analysis. From that information, the age and general health of the polar bear would be determined.

The team of scientists walked back to the snowmobile. Jake said, "I wish there were some other way — other than removing the tooth. That bear is still bleeding."

Josh countered, "No other way. We either have to cause polar bears pain and remove the back tooth for analysis, or the polar bear will become extinct."

INTERPRETING the scenario

1. DO JAKE AND JOSH CONSIDER THEIR JOB A WORTHWHILE CONTRIBUTION TO SOCIETY?

2. WHAT ATTITUDES DO JOSH AND JAKE HOLD TOWARDS PAIN?

3. DO JAKE AND JOSH FEEL PEOPLE ARE SUPERIOR TO THE ANIMALS?

4. WHAT DO YOU THINK OF THEIR SCIENTIFIC METHODS?

5. DO YOU THINK JOSH AND JAKE WILL CONTINUE TO WORK AS PARTNERS?

Read and Interpret a Scenario

✱ The philosophy of a person or culture can be judged by ✱ the attitudes held and the actions performed.

Directions: Read the SCENARIO. Consider the INTERPRETATION items.

The SCENARIO MOODS

The teacher took one look at Billy and knew: This was **not** going to be an easy day.

From the look on Billy's face, the teacher knew that Billy was in his "anti-social" mood. He wouldn't smile. He wouldn't talk. He wouldn't work. He would, most likely, kick and yell when told he had to do assignments.

"I don't have to smile at anybody!" Billy had yelled. "I don't have to like any of you! And I don't!"

INTERPRETING the scenario

1. DOES BILLY FEEL AN OBLIGATION TO THE REST OF THE WORLD?

2. WHAT SHOULD THE TEACHER DO?

3. WHY DOES BILLY HOLD THIS ATTITUDE?

4. DO YOU THINK BILLY BELIEVES WHAT HE SAYS?

5. IS A PERSON NATURALLY "SOCIAL" OR "ANTI-SOCIAL"?

Six Philosophers

IDEALISM—a theory that things exist only in the mind.

Immanuel Kant Born____ Died____ Country of Birth__________

One fact: ____

____

Arthur Schopenhauer Born____ Died____ Country of Birth________

One fact: ____

____

Henri Bergson Born____ Died____ Country of Birth__________

One fact: ____

____

RATIONALISM—a theory that knowledge comes only from logical and deductive reasoning.

Rene Descartes Born____ Died____ Country of Birth __________

One fact: ____

____

Gottfried W. Leibniz Born____ Died____ Country of Birth________

One fact: ____

____

Baruch Spinoza Born____ Died____ Country of Birth __________

One fact: ____

____

Leadership

A leader must "Lead Self; Lead Others"

A leader must rely upon
personal insights.

A leader must forge together different
schools of thought.

Directions:
    Describe what a leader could learn from each "...ism". The first is completed.

HEDONISM—a theory that tells people to seek pleasure.

People who are satisfied – sufficient food, clothes, pleasure – are sometimes easily fooled or easily lead

EMPIRICISM—a theory that all knowledge comes from experience.

NATURALISM—a theory that everything is natural and that nothing exists outside of nature.

Name: Immanuel Kant

Biographical Information:

1724-1804
Born in Königsberg in East Prussia (now Russia).

Contribution to Philosophy:

As an adult, Kant was about five feet tall and had a deformed shoulder. He never traveled. He taught near Konigsberg from 1746 to 1755. Then he taught at the University of Konigsberg until his death nearly fifty years later.

He led a very punctual methodical life: rising daily at five, eating at 1:00, and going for an hour's walk every afternoon at 4:00.

CRITIQUE OF PURE REASON is his chief written work. In it, Kant discussed the limits of human knowledge. Kant argued that the mind organizes experiences into definite patterns. It is those patterns that we know.

He held definite viewpoints on ethics. Two of these viewpoints are:
1. Doing one's duty is more important than being happy or making others happy.
2. Even if scientists predict certain occurrences, man has free will.

Kant thought that the best thing in the world is good will — the will to follow the right way regardless of what happens to ourselves.

"Do not be concerned about your happiness. Just do your duty."

"Two things fill the mind with ever new and increasing wonder and awe — the starry heavens above me and the moral law within me."

22

Name: *G.W.F. Hegel*

Biographical Information:

1770–1831
George Wilhelm Friedrich Hegel was born in Stuttgart, Germany.

Contribution to Philosophy:

G.W.F. Hegel wanted to develop a system of philosophy in which all the contributions of predecessors would be integrated.

Hegel believed that the world operates according to reason. We can understand the world only if we attune our own individual reason to the reason of the universe.

His first book, THE PHENOMENOLOGY OF THE SPIRIT, stated that viewpoints are just so many states of mind. Each viewpoint is a development towards maturity.

Hegel believed that reality is constantly changing.

He thought that everything contradicts itself. All things have a ''plus'' and a ''minus'' quality which war against each other. Out of this struggle between pluses and minuses, comes growth and eventual union.

The plus is called ''thesis''.

The minus is called ''antithesis''.

The union is called ''synthesis''.

After Hegel's death, his students published his lectures on the philosophy of history, religion, and art.

Read and Interpret a Scenario

The philosophy of a person or culture can be judged by the attitudes held and the actions performed.

Directions:

Read the SCENARIO. Consider the INTERPRETATION items.

The SCENARIO *MONEY*

The coins were heavy in her pocket.
"I'll count them when I go into the basement," Lelani thought to herself. "No one will see me in the basement."

In the far corner of the basement, where Lelani kept her things, she counted the coins.

For sometime, Lelani had been stealing coins from other children at school. Her pile of coins was growing. She would soon have enough to buy some really neat clothes.

She thought to herself, "I only take the money from rich kids. They won't miss it. I'm poor. I have a right to the money from the rich kids."

Lelani hid the money. She didn't want her mom to find it. Her mother didn't understand about special clothes for school. Her mother didn't agree that rich kids had more money than they needed.

INTERPRETING the scenario

1. IS STEALING EVER JUSTIFIED?

2. WHY ARE 'NEAT CLOTHES' SO IMPORTANT TO LELANI? SHOULD THEY BE?

3. DO LELANI AND HER MOTHER HAVE SIMILAR ATTITUDES TOWARDS 'NEAT CLOTHES' AND RICH PEOPLE?

Read and Interpret a Scenario

> *The philosophy of a person or culture can be judged by the attitudes held and the actions performed.*

Directions: Read the SCENARIO. Consider the INTERPRETATION items.

The SCENARIO Guns

The guns were there: all of them. There were short ones and long ones, decorated and plain ones. Some were for specific uses; others served multi-purpose needs. But all were guns — capable of wounding and killing.

INTERPRETING the scenario

1. IS IT A "RIGHT" OF EVERY PERSON TO OWN AND OPERATE A GUN?

2. DOES EVERY "RIGHT" HAVE A "RESPONSIBILITY"?

3. CAN YOU LEGISLATE RESPONSIBLE BEHAVIOR?

4. IS THERE, OR CAN THERE BE, A UNIVERSALLY-ACCEPTED CODE OF BEHAVIOR?

5. IF THERE WERE NO GUNS, WOULD THE WORLD BE AT PEACE?

Name: *John Dewey*

Biographical Information:

1859–1952.   Burlington, Vermont   United States
His father kept a country store in Burlington, Vermont.

Contribution to Philosophy:

John Dewey was influenced by the American democratic way of life and by the new science of psychology.

Dewey believed that intelligence is a power that people use when faced with conflict or challenge. He also believed that people live by habits and customs.

He wrote widely on art, democracy, education, philosophy, and science. All of his writings focus on how to close the distance between thought and action.

He encouraged the notion of pragmatism. Pragmatism is a belief that the correctness or incorrectness of action should be judged by the results obtained from that action.

Dewey believed that knowledge is a means of controlling the environment.

In education, he encouraged experimentation as a method of learning.

Students should learn about current issues and problems. To be complete, education must include the daily glorious, joyous, sad, tedious, boring, terrifying, and tragic experiences of life. His notion of education came to be called ''Progressive Education''.

Many practices of schools are based on Dewey's principles.

Name: *Bertrand Russell*

Biographical Information:

```
1872-1970.   Born near Trelleck, Wales.
His family was active in politics and public life.
```

Contribution to Philosophy:

Russell believed that philosophical ideas are both the cause and effect of historical trends and attitudes. He believed philosophical thoughts are directly related to politics.

Russell always championed the cause of individual liberty and freedom. He urged people to do away with superstition, violence, and suppression of thought. He opposed tyrannies that tried to control minds.

In 1950, he won the Nobel prize in literature for his writings which defended humanity and freedom of thought.

During World War I, he was dismissed from Cambridge University and imprisoned because of his pacifist views.

In the early 1960's, Russell led pacifist movements to ban nuclear weapons. He was imprisoned briefly in 1962 for these activities.

Russell wrote over 40 books. One of his books is WISDOM OF THE WEST.

He taught at many universities, including: Harvard, Peking (China), Chicago, California, Cambridge (England).

> *"It is clear that thought is not free if the profession of certain opinions make it impossible to earn a living."*
>
> *"Tolerance is a pre-requisite in a society in which inquiry is to flourish."*

Read and Interpret a Scenario.

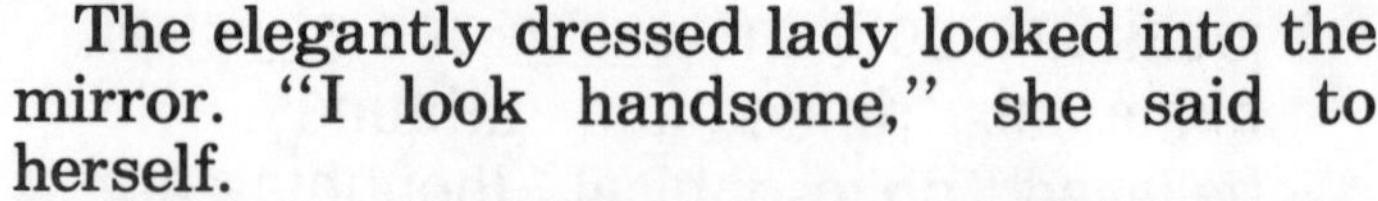

⭐ *The philosophy of a person or culture can be judged by the attitudes held and the actions performed.* ⭐

Directions: Read the SCENARIO.

The SCENARIO. *Aging*

The elegantly dressed lady looked into the mirror. "I look handsome," she said to herself.

And she was handsome. Her hair was pulled back in a soft dignified style which accented the high blushed cheekbones. With the pearl earrings, her face looked confident and competent.

"I hope I never look any older than I do today," she said. But no one was there to hear her.

As she walked past the dining room buffet, she noticed a picture of her mother. Her mother looked confident, competent and old. Her smiling face was creased. Her hair no longer held a hairdo. She wore outdated glasses and very little makeup. "I'll just be myself," her mother had said.

INTERPRETING the scenario.

WRITE ONE QUESTION FOR DISCUSSION

____

____

Read and Interpret a Scenario

The philosophy of a person or culture can be judged by the attitudes held and the actions performed.

Directions: Read the SCENARIO. Consider the INTERPRETATION items.

The SCENARIO *A Birthday*

Grandpa and Grandma are smiling. They, like me, want today to be special. It is my birthday. I want all of us to be happy. I want Grandpa and Grandma to be happy.

Being happy doesn't happen very often these days.

After a lot of yelling and being mean to all of us, my parents divorced. Sure, I know. It happens every day. So, what's the big deal?

The "big deal" is that it happened to **me**, me—Rosa! I cried a lot. I guess maybe Grandma and Grandpa cried, too.

But, today, we **will** all be happy. I'll **make** us be happy. I'll make mom and dad stop yelling at each other long enough to smile, to eat cake, and be civil. I'll see to it that Grandma and Grandpa keep that smile.

INTERPRETING the scenario

1. DOES ROSA BELIEVE A FAMILY SHOULD BE HAPPY TOGETHER?

2. WHAT ROLE DO YOU THINK GRANDMA AND GRANDPA PLAY IN THE LIFE OF ROSA?

3. IS DIVORCE A <u>SOLUTION</u> TO A PROBLEM, OR IS IT THE <u>SOURCE</u> OF A PROBLEM?

Existentialism

It is easy to see how a philosophy such as existentialism would develop.

The history of Europe in the 1800's and 1900's is filled with an immense amount of human cruelty and suffering. The occurrence of human cruelty and suffering has continued throughout the 20th century. The existentialist philosophers continue to seek meaning and value for lives which often appear to have no meaning.

Existentialists see human life as a series of decisions made by each individual person. The person can rely upon no one but self.

The bright positive side of existentialism is that it maintains and upholds the dignity and free will of the individual. The dark disquieting side is freedom.

How can freedom be dark and disquieting? Freedom can be an enormously heavy burden. To the existentialist, ''freedom'' is the absolute responsibility one must take for every single action, thought, or omission. One cannot ''blame'' God, church, society, friends, culture...for any decision that one makes.

Existentialists do not consider themselves a religion or a major body of philosophy. Rather, their ideas are often presented through the actions they take and the writings they publish: nonfiction articles, fictional stories, novels, plays and poetry.

In their works, existentialists concentrate on the extremes of the human condition: prison camps, suicide, starvation... They feel that by admitting and dealing with the worst, people can better face the lesser crises of each day.

All existentialist philosophers do not agree on the same ideas. However, they are all vitally concerned with the value or purpose of human existence.

 # *EXISTENTIALIST Philosophers* 

> **EXISTENTIALISM** grew out of the works of two thinkers of the 1800s:
> Søren Kierkegaard, a Danish philosopher
> Friedrich Nietzsche, a German philosopher

OTHER PROMINENT EXISTENTIALISTS

SIMONE DE BEAUVOIR	MARTIN BUBER	MARTIN HEIDEGGER	GABRIEL MARCEL
NICOLAS BERDYAEV	ALBERT CAMUS	KARL JASPERS	JEAN-PAUL SARTRE

Read about several existentialist philosophers.
Give some information about each.
Share the information with others.

Name: ____

Biographical Information: ____

Contribution to Philosophy: ____

____

Name: ____

Biographical Information: ____

Contribution to Philosophy: ____

____

Name: ____

Biographical Information: ____

Contribution to Philosophy: ____

____

31

Twelve Eternal Questions

People have pondered these questions for centuries. But each individual must answer these questions if each is to find meaning in life.

<u>Be tolerant of individual viewpoints.</u>

Discuss:

1. Why am I here?

2. What is evil?

3. Why is evil in the world?

4. What is the relationship between individual freedom and the rights of others?

5. Are we free?

6. Should we be free?

7. What is my obligation towards myself?

8. What is my obligation towards the rest of the world?

9. Are people inherently good or evil?

10. Of what value is a living plant, animal, or human being?

11. Is there a master plan for the universe?

12. Are we masters of our own destiny?

More Questions

Directions:
List other questions that you have.
If possible, discuss the answers to your questions.

____

____

____

____

____

____

____

____

____

____

____

____

____

____

____

____

____

____

____

Be tolerant of the opinions of others. You need not agree with what others say, nor do others have to agree with you.

Read and Interpret a Scenario.

 # The philosophy of a person or culture can be judged by #
the attitudes held and the actions performed.

The SCENARIO: Time

The room was full of clocks. Each was giving
a message.

Time heals all wounds.

Time marches on.

Time waits for no one.

The greatest gift I can give you is my time.

Each second of time comes but once. Don't waste it.

INTERPRETING the scenario.

INTERPRETATION items.

____
____
____
____
____

Completing Quotations

Directions: Complete each quotation. List author of the quotation.

"The unexamined life is *not worth living.* " SOCRATES
author

1. "A sound mind in _______________________________ "
author

2. "Tolerance is a pre-requisite in a society in which

_______________________________ . "
author

3. "Do not be concerned about your happiness.

_______________________________ . "
author

4. "I think; _______________________________ . "
author

5. "Those having torches

_______________________________ . "
author

6. "Two things fill the mind with ever new and increasing   wonder and awe —

____

_______________________________ . "
author

7. "I am not an Athenian nor a Greek,

_______________________________ . "
author

8. "It is clear that thought is not free if the profession of

____

_______________________________ . "
author

9. "We should have a great many fewer disputes in the world
   if words were taken for what they are, the signs of our

_______________________________ . "
author

10. "Philosophy is _______________________________ "
author

A List of Philosophers

Abelard, Peter
Adams, Henry Brooks
Alcott, Bronson
Anaxagoras
Anaximander
Anaximenes
Aurelius, Marcus

Bacon, Francis
Bacon, Roger
Bayle, Pierre
Bentham, Jeremy
Berkeley, George
Bradley, Francis H.
Bergson, Henri
Berdyaev, Nicolas

Carneades
Comte, Auguste
Condorcet, Marquis de
Confucius
Croce, Benedetto

Democritus
Descartes, Rene
Dewey, John
Diderot, Denis
Diogenes
Durant, Will

Emerson, Ralph W.
Epictetus
Epicurus
Erasmus, Desiderius

Feurerbach, Ludwig
Fichte, Johann G.
Fiske, John

Hegel, George W.F.
Heidegger, Martin
Heraclitus
Herbart, Johann F.
Herder, Johann G.
Hobbes, Thomas
Hsun-tzu
Hume, David

Iqbal, Sir Muhammed

James, William
Jaspers, Karl

Kant, Immanuel
Kierkegaard, Søren A.

Leibniz, Gottfried W.
Locke, John
Lotze, Rudolf H.
Lucretius

Marcel, Gabriel
Maimonides
Marx, Karl
Mill, John Stuart
Mumford, Lewis

Nietzsche, Friedrich
Nageli, Karl W.

Ortega y Gasset, Jose

Pascal, Blaise
Pierce, Charles S.
Plato
Plotinus
Pyrrho of Elis
Pythagoras

Rosenberg, Alfred
Royce, Josiah
Rousseau, Jean Jacques
Russell, Bertrand

Santayana, George
Sartre, Jean-Paul
Schelling, Friedrich
Schopenhauer, Arthur
Schweitzer, Albert
Seneca, Lucius A.
Socrates
Spencer, Herbert
Spengler, Oswald
Spinoza, Baruch

Tagore, Sir Rabindranath
Thales
Thoreau, Henry D.
Tocqueville, Alexis de
Tolstoy, Leo N.
Tyndall, John

Unamuno, Miguel de
Voltaire

Whitehead, Alfred N.
William of Ockham
Wittgenstein, Ludwig
Wundt, Wilhelm
Zeno

PHILOSOPHER'S
Name: ____________________

Biographical Information:

____

____

Contribution to Philosophy:

____

____

____

____

____

____

____

____

____

____

____

____

____

____

Left margin (top to bottom): Jaspers, Karl · Unamuno, Miguel de · Comte, Auguste · Kierkegaard, Søren A. · Confucius

Right margin (top to bottom): Locke, John · Voltaire · Zeno · Dewey, John · Thales · Socrates · Hegel, George W.F.

Read and Interpret a Scenario

The philosophy of a person or culture can be judged by the attitudes held and the actions performed.

Directions:
WRITE *the SCENARIO.*   SUGGEST *the INTERPRETATION items.*

The SCENARIO   TITLE _________________________

INTERPRETING the scenario

Planning Sheet for Individual Project

Student name _________________________   Planning Date _________________________

A. Type of project: (circle one)   report   drama   poster   sketch   flashcards

other ____

B. Title of Project

____

____

C. What the project will look like or be when it is completed (as now "seen" in the mind of the planner). Continue on reverse side if more room is needed.

____

____

____

D. Plan of Procedure (continue on reverse side of page if more room is needed):

____

____

____

____

____

★ ★ ★ ★ ★ ★ ★ ★ ★ ★ ★ ★ ★ ★ ★ ★

E. This project was not completed because _______________________________________
        or
This project was completed and reviewed by _____________________________________
                                              (name of person or group)

F. Comments by student completing project: _____________________________________

Project was (circle one):   very satisfying   satisfying   could have been better

G. Comments by teacher/mentor: ____

Project was (circle one):   excellent   satisfactory   could have been better

_______________________________   _______________________________________
Student signature   Date   Teacher/mentor signature   Date

1. Read a biography of a philosopher.

2. Make a poster showing themes of an existentialist philosopher.

3. Make a collection of flash cards listing a quotation on one side and the source of the quotation on the other.

4. Write an essay on the issue that greatly concerns you.

5. Pretend you are a well-known philosopher. Prepare and perform a "one-person show" based on the writings/ideas of that philosopher.

6. Write a play in which 3 (or more) philosophers discuss a certain issue.

7. Make a timeline showing the philosophers studied in this program. If you wish, add other philosophers.

8. If you could interview a philosopher studied in this program, what questions would you ask? Prepare three or more questions.

9. All philosophers listed in this course are men. Were there women philosophers? Research the topic.

10. Write an essay that begins:

I think the study of philosophy is...

Student Projects

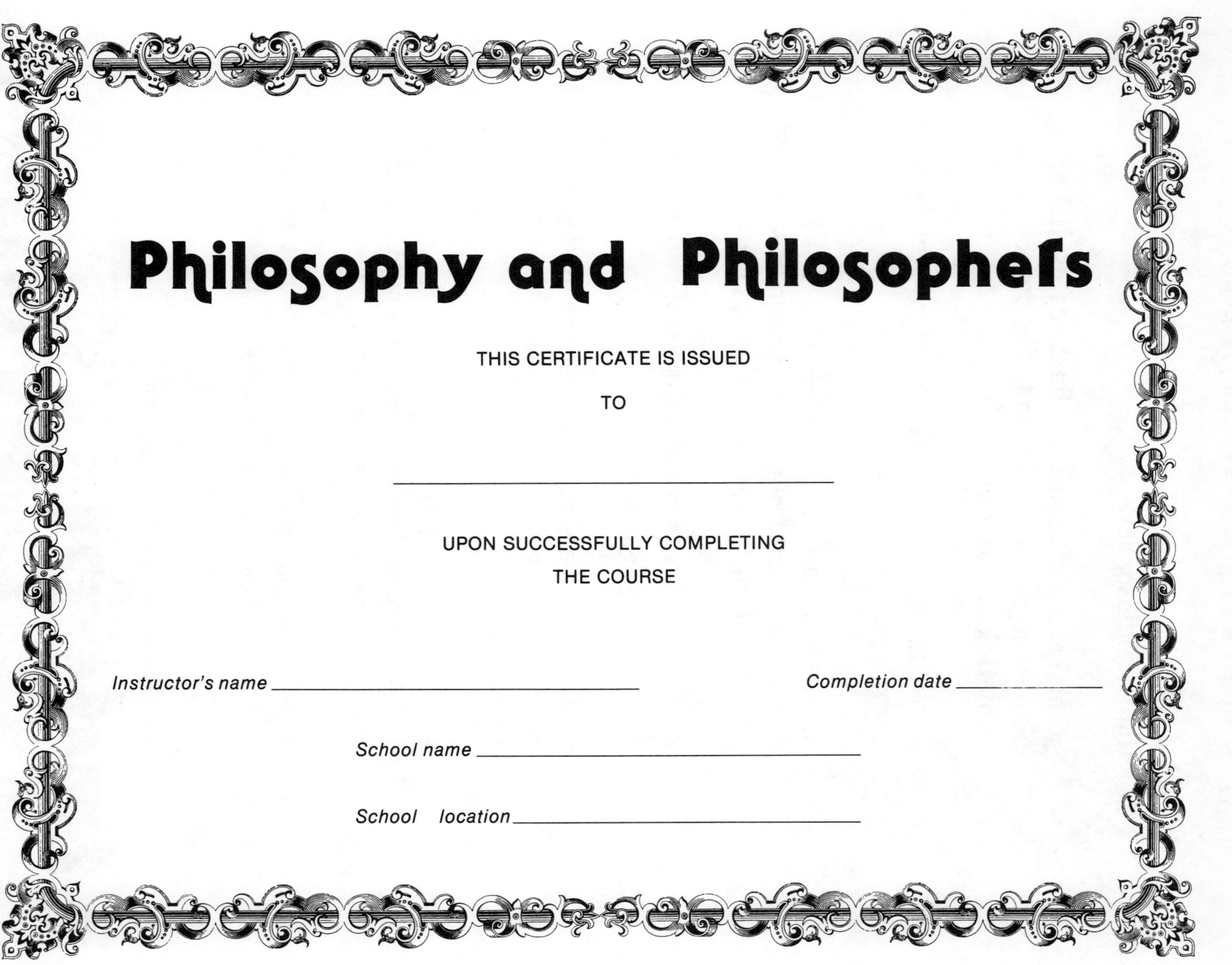

Philosophy and Philosophers

THIS CERTIFICATE IS ISSUED

TO

____

UPON SUCCESSFULLY COMPLETING

THE COURSE

Instructor's name _________________________________   Completion date _______________

School name _____________________________________

School   location _________________________________

PHILOSOPHY AND PHILOSOPHERS

OBJECTIVES:

1. To provide information about major philosophical schools of thought.

2. To acquaint students with philosophers and their contribution to philosophical thought.

3. To provide opportunities for discussion of philosophical questions posed by the students.

4. To install and encourage in young students a love of wisdom which will carry into adult life.

BEFORE USING THIS INSTRUCTIONAL PROGRAM, THE INSTRUCTOR SHOULD:

1. Read and study each page of this instructional program.

2. Select the pages to be used. (Adapt the program each time it is taught.)

3. Read several philosophy books and/or a biography of a philosopher.

4. Prepare oneself mentally for the diversity of ideas which will be expressed during the class sessions.

PHILOSOPHERS INCLUDED IN THIS BOOK

Philosophers included in this book are philosophers who:

1. are well-accepted in the field of philosophy, and/or

2. have made a unique contribution to philosophical thought.

In no way are the philosophers included in this instructional program meant to cover all important philosophers. Philosophers selected for this book cover many centuries, represent different schools of thought, come from different countries, and are understandable to young learners. Students may include information on other philosophers.

USING THIS PROGRAM

Note: This instructional program should not necessarily be taught in the page-by-page sequence of this book. Arrange the contents and sequence of the program to match the learning needs and styles of students taking this philosophy course.

Page-by-page Suggestions

PAGE 1. DEFINITION OF PHILOSOPHY
Read. Encourage student to memorize definition.

PAGE 2. READ AND INTERPRET A SCENARIO: *The Party*
Follow the directions on the page. Permit much discussion.

PAGE 3. THE GOLDEN RULE.

PAGE 4. BIOGRAPHICAL SKETCH: Confucius.

PAGE 5. THE PHILOSOPHERS: ATTITUDES AND TOOLS
Philosophers cannot be put into a stereotypical category.
However, many philosophers share common attitudes and tools.

Other attitudes could include:
   -strong sense of purpose in life,
   -belief that circumstances or attitudes can change,
   -conviction that their way of thinking is the correct way,
   ...others...
Other tools could be:

   -analysis, conjecture, imagination, listening, ...

PAGE 6. READ AND INTERPRET A SCENARIO: *The Prairie* .

PAGE 7. READ AND INTERPRET A SCENARIO: *Heritage.*

PAGE 8. READ AND INTERPRET A SCENARIO : *Death.*

PAGE 9. BIOGRAPHICAL SKETCH: Socrates.

PAGE 10. BIOGRAPHICAL SKETCH: Plato.

PAGE 11. BIOGRAPHICAL SKETCH : Aristotle.

PAGES 12, 13. THE "...ISMS" AND THE "...OLOGIES".

   Student answers will vary.

PAGE 14. AXIOLOGY : EDUCATION.
   Student answers will vary.

PAGE 15. MATCHING ...OLOGIES AND ...ISMS.

1. hedonism	2. realism	3. ideology
4. empiricism	5. cosmology	6. psychology
7. rationalism	8. axiology	9. naturalism
10. astrology	11. epistemology	12. idealism
13. ontology		

PAGE 16. BIOGRAPHICAL SKETCH : Rene Descartes.

PAGE 17. BIOGRAPHICAL SKETCH: John Locke.

> Do not moralize or preach to your students. This is neither the time, nor place, nor setting.

PAGE 18. READ AND INTERPRET A SCENARIO : *Polar Bears.*

PAGE 19. READ AND INTERPRET A SCENARIO: *Moods.*

PAGE 20. SIX PHILOSOPHERS.
Accept factual information students give.
Verifying sources of information should be reviewed.

Birth, Death, Country of Birth Information:

KANT: 1724 - 1804. East Prussia (now Russia).

SCHOPENAUER: 1788 - 1860. Germany.

BERGSON: 1859 - 1941. France.

DESCARTES: 1596 - 1650. France.

LEIBNIZ: 1646 - 1716. Germany.

SPINOZA: 1632 - 1677. Netherlands.

PAGE 21. LEADERSHIP AND PHILOSOPHY.

Student answers will vary.
Some suggestions:
People influenced by empiricism believe:
research findings, their own experiences, observations.
A leader appealing to an empirically-minded person
could appeal to: research data, past history...

People influenced by naturalism believe:
events happen with little or no intervention,
reality can be observed, nature runs its course, ...
A leader appealing to a naturalistic-minded person
could appeal to the integrity of natural selection,
priority of local concerns, and praise for
individuals within a group, ...

PAGE 22. BIOGRAPHICAL SKETCH: Immanuel Kant.

PAGE 23. BIOGRAPHICAL SKETCH: George Wilhelm Friedrich Hegel.

PAGE 24. READ AND INTERPRET A SCENARIO: *Money.*

PAGE 25. READ AND INTERPRET A SCENARIO : *Guns.*

PAGE 26. BIOGRAPHICAL SKETCH: John Dewey.

PAGE 27. BIOGRAPHICAL SKETCH: Bertrand Russell.

PAGE 28. READ AND INTERPRET A SCENARIO: *Aging.*

PAGE 29. READ AND INTERPRET A SCENARIO: *A Birthday.*

PAGE 30. EXISTENIALISM - A PHILOSOPHICAL SCHOOL OF THOUGHT.

PAGE 31. EXISTENIALISTS.
   Limited information is given here - for quick teacher reference.
      SIMONE DE BEAUVOIR- 1908 -   French author.
      NICOLAS BERDYAEV -   1874 - 1948. Russian religious and political thinker.
      MARTIN BUBER - 1878 - 1965. Jewish philosopher and Zionist leader.
      ALBERT CAMUS - 1913 - 1960. French journalist, novelist, essayist,playwright.
      MARTIN HEIDEGGER - 1889 - 1976. German philosopher.
      KARL JASPERS - 1883 - 1969. German philosopher.
      GABRIEL MARCEL - 1889 - 1973. French philosopher.
      JEAN-PAUL SARTRE - 1905 - 1980. French writer of novels, plays and stories.

PAGES 32,33, 34.   TWELVE ETERNAL QUESTIONS. MORE QUESTIONS.
   Permit much discussion on topics listed pages 32,33.
   Students write their own questions on page 34.

PAGE 36. COMPLETING QUOTATIONS.

   1. ... a sound body." Socrates.
   2. ... inquiry is to flourish." B.Russell.
   3. ... Just do your duty." Kant.
   4. ...therefore I am. " Descartes.
   5. ...will pass them on to others." Plato.
   6. ... - the starry heavens above me and the moral law within me." Kant.
   7. ...but a citizen of the world." Socrates.
   8. ...certain opinions make it impossible to earn a living." Russell.
   9. ... ideas only, and not for things themselves." Locke.
   10. ... the highest music." Plato.

PAGE 37. LIST OF PHILOSOPHERS.

PAGE 38. BIOGRAPHICAL REPORT- OPEN FORM.

PAGE 39. READ AND INTERPRET A SCENARIO - OPEN FORM.

PAGE 40. PLANNING SHEET FOR INDIVIDUAL STUDENT PROJECT - OPEN FORM.

PAGE 41. STUDENT PROJECTS - IDEAS.

PAGE 42. CERTIFICATE OF COMPLETION.